WIN NO MATTER WHAT

WIN NO MATTER WHAT

Be the Best When Life is at Its Worst.

SUZANNE EVANS

Dedicated to Adrien, who always knows the score.

Published by
Hybrid Global Publishing
301 E 57th Street
4th Floor
New York, NY 10022

Manufactured in the United States of America.

Evans, Suzanne

Win No Matter What: Be the Best When Life is at Its Worst.
　　ISBN: 978-1-951943-85-1
　　eBook: 978-1-951943-86-8

Cover design by: Branding For The People
Copyediting by: XCU Agency
Interior design by: Suba Murugan
Author photo by: Lesley Bohm

Legal Disclaimer:
If you know or suspect you have a health problem, it is recommended you seek your medical or mental health professional's advice.

www.driveninc.com

CONTENTS

Life Is Like Business—Chaotic

Life is messy. It is pandemonium. It is steeped in disorder.

It requires courage, grit, and being comfortable with being uncomfortable.

(I know, not the most inspiring message to start a book.)

Why are we starting here?

Because it's important to acknowledge that to be part of the human race means to live in perpetual conflict. To know that we are *always* just two moments away from a potential crisis, and most of our time is spent solving one while simultaneously working to prevent the next.

To be clear, a crisis isn't a bad thing. A crisis teaches us to focus, to get our shit together, and solve whatever is upon us because at that moment—we have no other choice. A crisis can be cleansing as it forces us to look at whatever problems we are facing in the eye and decide whether we want to address them and ultimately solve them or stay in a perpetual state of disarray.

People who succeed in the world don't actively avoid conflict and crisis, but they work to solve them when they land on their doorstep. Those who find themselves feeling as though they are in a perpetual loop of crisis (or, more clearly, reliving the same situation over and over again) do so because they fail to address the root cause.

The point of it all is: Crisis and conflict are constantly swooping in and out of our lives because they are what comes with being alive.

(Yeah, some of you are saying, "I don't have any crises or conflicts in my life," and I'm here to tell you that you're full of shit. The only people I know who don't have any problems to contend with are, quite simply, dead.)

So while living with crises is part of the game, everyone experiencing a crisis at the exact same time rarely ever happens. That's what makes this past year and a half so fascinating; the entire planet was experiencing an unprecedented health crisis for the first time in modern human history. For the first time, nearly everyone was required to stay indoors, cut themselves off from the majority of the people they love, and find new ways to work, live, and communicate. As a result, we watched businesses close, people suffer mental health issues, people get sick and pass away, and many other problems that we are still trying to make sense of.

It was, in short, chaotic. At least at first.

This is not a book about COVID-19.

It was, however, written during the year and a half that I, like all of you, was quarantined at home during COVID-19.

This is a short book with a big message.

I wrote it because the way many people behaved during the pandemic illustrates how they acted even before it began. Many of those who had their shit together kept it together (even with some struggle). Those who didn't—saw many of their problems exacerbated. And some people—who were struggling before the pandemic—were able to use that time to grow, learn, and become a better version of themselves.

This is a book for all of them.

The lessons in it were taken from my experiences and the experiences of my personal friends and clients and are meant to illustrate that no matter what takes place in your life, crisis is inevitable. What's not inevitable is how we respond to it.

In this book, I aim to show you the path to thrive regardless of what life throws at you, how to stay focused when conflict and crisis arrive, and how to kick ass when things are quiet. I'm here to remind you that everyone has some form of chaos in their lives at all times. I promise you—it's not just you. So I'm here to challenge you, make you think, and ultimately, help you take action.

Action is what's most important. It's what keeps you focused. It's what keeps you motivated.

It's what makes you win.

CHAPTER 1

Winners Love to Play the Game

"I play the game for the game's own sake."
– Arthur Conan Doyle, as Sherlock Holmes

Before we begin, there are a few things you should know about me:

I like to play.

I like to win.

I like to play even when I have no chance of winning.

Oh, and I never lose.

Not because I always win. But because I always *play* until the buzzer runs out.

And I *never* quit until someone literally pulls me off the court.

"Unless it's bleeding, keep playing."
That was my mama's motto back when she was my basketball coach. You see, she taught me early on that you stay in the game, and you stay in the fight unless you are physically unable to keep playing. No matter how bad the pain is, it will be fine if you keep playing. When life seems overwhelming, challenging, scary, or painful, it will all be fine; keep playing.

When a global pandemic erupts and fundamentally changes every aspect of our life as we know it, disrupting the way we live, the way we connect with others, and for the purposes of you reading this book, the way our businesses operate—we have two options:

1. We quit.
2. We keep playing.

WHAT KIND OF PLAYER ARE YOU?
We're jumping right into this, okay? You need to decide **right now** what type of player you are and if you're willing to do what it takes to win, regardless of the circumstances you are facing. Whether it's a global pandemic or losing a loved one or the risk of foreclosure, you've got to decide if you want to play like a winner or play like someone trying not to lose.

Understand me: I'm not implying that the past year hasn't been terrifying. I'm not saying that the stakes haven't been higher than ever. I'm not saying it hasn't felt as though we've been fighting a war for survival. We have. But I also know that feeling as though you are fighting a battle every day can wreak havoc on one's sanity. And this is why I believe you have to treat the current state of our world as a game. You've got to treat it as a game. You've got to play it like a game.

Because once you recognize that this is all a game, your next step is to look at what this game looks like, what you need to be doing, who you need to be, and how you need to show up to win.

As we look back at how the past year and a half has unfolded, it's often felt as though things were getting worse before they were getting better.

If you play not to lose, the odds are that you do whatever you can to try and prevent things from completely falling apart as a situation gets worse.

But when you play to win, you can decide that as the situation gets worse, you can get better.

When you play to win, you can get smarter with each passing day. You can get more innovative. More creative. You can listen to your clients in a better way and understand what they need, not what you're hoping they'll buy from you.

Are You Ready to Play to Win?

When you play to win, you become more disciplined. You learn to make better decisions. You learn to let go of the emotional, irrational, short-term decisions that will only result in long-term disasters. You'll say in your lane; you'll be more focused.

And that all begins with knowing how to prepare your mind for winning this new game in our new normal.

PREPARING YOUR MIND

1. I want you to think back over the past year (I get that our first impulse is to pretend that 2020 never happened, but tap into that bravery) and ask yourself what was the first thought you had every morning.

Did you wake up with a pit in your stomach?

Did you say to yourself, "Oh no, things are getting worse"?

Did you wonder how your business would continue to survive when it seemed like everything was falling apart?

If you did, you were preparing your mind to live in scarcity.

You were preparing your mind to live in suffering.

You were giving your brain carte blanche to spread anxiety all over the place.

And when you live in that place, the odds are things do get worse because you were expecting it.

Let me share how I wake up every day.
I wake up every morning expecting shit to go sideways. I expect problems to emerge. I expect that something will show up on my desk that I could never have planned for but must have a plan to deal with. "Oh yeah, that's what I thought. I knew something like this could happen. So how can I change how I'm playing to make this work?"

Do you see the difference?
The first approach that so many people take is to see the downside of any situation immediately. They let the situation determine their reaction. My approach is to be proactive. Always. I remember, it's a game, and I have to wake up each day expecting *shit to go down, but never let it get me down.*

Suppose we train our minds to understand that we are actually playing a game, and we learn to love to play the game for the game's own sake. In that case, we can learn to work smarter, be more disciplined, work better, and remain calm regardless of what is happening.

2. Are you playing offense or defense?
The next step in preparing your mind to always win is to ask yourself if you're playing offense or defense (this is another clever way of asking if you're playing to win or not to lose).

This. Is. Huge.

When we're in the midst of a crisis, our first inclination is to play defense. Don't.

When things are getting crazy, it's the perfect time to play offense. It's the ideal time to attack the ball. The ball is the prize at this moment.

Offense is about scoring points.

It's about making big, strategic plays.

It's about going after the right things and doubling your efforts.

It's about watching the competition and seeing what they are doing and making sure to zig when they zag.

Here's what happens when you play defense.
When you play defense, you're tentative.

You're telling yourself, "Gosh, I hope this works. I hope this passes. Maybe I can stop this thing from falling apart. Maybe I can minimize the damage."

You can't afford to be a defensive player in a crisis.

You can't curl up in a ball of fear and wish this shit away.

You can't try to keep things the way they've always been.

Why? Because the fucking world has changed.

Your business is no longer what it once was.

Your personal life, family life, and social life—nothing is the same as it used to be.

If you're playing offense, you're taking a fresh approach.
You're creative. You're going after the ball. You're using this opportunity to try new shit and seeing if it works. You're maintaining your focus while everyone else is distracted. You're keeping your eyes on the prize when everyone else is overwhelmed.

If you can play offense, you can use this time to help your business win the game by being there for your clients in ways the competition can't.

PLAYING OFFENSE — BEST PRACTICES

Playing to win requires a little bit of being able to outlast, outwit, and outsmart. You'll have to outsmart everything; you'll need to develop the ability to cut through all the white noise that's going on around you.

You also have to listen. Listen to where your clients and customers are right now. Recognize that everyone is in a different place. Everyone around you is processing the past year differently and in their unique way. This means you can't shove your business down other people's throats, no matter how good your offer is.

Listen to where your clients are and meet them there.
Listen to what they need and what they are asking for and offer them that.

In times like these, what worked in the past won't work in the present.

Master the art of adaptation.
You will need to learn to adapt. Whatever your business, you can no longer run it as you did before. You must adapt to the new reality. Adapt your services. Adapt your offerings. Adapt how you conduct business. Lean into the reality, read the room, and be willing to say, "No problem, we're going to make this work for you because it sounds like this is what you need right now."

Adapt. Innovate. Survive. But remember...

It's not survival of the fittest. It's survival of the most useful.
This is a lesson whether you are a business owner or even an employee. When tough times hit our doorsteps, those who provide the most value and the most use are the ones who will survive. The employees who are "head down, heart up" and doing the work, making sure that they are everything that their colleagues need and that their business needs and their managers need—these are the employees who are going to survive. The business owners who ensure that their clients and their families have everything they need to stay afloat and feel supported are the ones who will endure.

Remember that silence is deafening for your business.
One of the biggest mistakes I saw entrepreneurs and business owners make during the pandemic was to go silent.

Now I get it. Whenever there's a big crisis, many of us can go in and out of knowing what to do, or more importantly, what to say. So many of us are afraid of saying something offensive or appearing ignorant that rather than talk about what is going on, we shut down because we think it's better not to make noise than to make noise that might ruffle some feathers.

The problem is that your silence is deafening to your potential customers, clients, and employees.

When you feel yourself being silent, you're in trouble. When you haven't connected with someone, you're in trouble.

When in doubt, shout it out.
You hear me? When in doubt, shout it out. I'll tell you what that means and what that looks like for me.

When I find myself going silent, I do what I do best; I share stuff with the world. I go online, on Facebook, on Instagram. I open my mouth, even if I'm not sure what the hell I am trying to say. I focus on what's easy for me.

What's easy for you?
When you find yourself going silent, go on the offensive and lean into what comes naturally. Is it talking about your fears? Is it talking about your business? Is it talking about your kids?

When in doubt, let me hear it. When in doubt, you...fill in the blank. You shout it out because silence is deafening. If you're silent, you're not connecting with enough people. If you're silent, you're not putting enough content out. Be smart about it. Be strategic about it. Be randomly all over the place. Choose your few mediums and then just flood them with content, great information, great ideas. Just do something, anything other than going silent. My ears can't take it.

80/20 moments
Maybe you have children or siblings or parents or friends or neighbors who are employees and feeling worried about the economy, about their job security. When you play offensively, you can talk to them about who they need to be and how they need to show up. It's okay to acknowledge that no one feels amazing and is tap dancing through their neighborhoods right now, but we don't have to feel good all the time. We just need to be positive 80 percent of the time. This is an 80/20 moment, isn't it? So all of us have to give ourselves a moment to go, "Shit," and give ourselves a moment to be upset, give ourselves a moment to freak out.

I have had my fair share of freak-out moments (I am human, after all). I've felt the fear and felt like crap and wanted to hang it all up. But here's the thing—I only allow myself to do it 20 percent of the time. The same goes for you.

You hear me? Twenty percent of the time. If it's happening more than 20 percent of the time, we're all going to be in trouble.

So figure out what your 20 percent is. Give yourself that 20 percent of the time to rest, be pissed off, and feel hopeless, frustrated, annoyed, and flabbergasted. But know that 80 percent of the time, you're going to be playing to win. Eighty percent of the time, you're going to be disciplined. Eighty percent of the time, you're sticking to your schedule. Your routine. Ensure that 80 percent of the time, you know precisely what you need to be doing to remain calm amongst the chaos happening in the world today or tomorrow.

You can do this. If you keep your head on straight, make good decisions, stay in action, stay smart, you will be more than okay—a hell of a lot more than okay. Sure, things won't look perfect. It will be messy as hell at times. But that 80 percent will make an enormous difference.

CHAPTER 2

You Need Problems

"Problems are nothing but wake-up calls for creativity."
— Gerhard Gschwandtner

It's all too much. It's too hard. It's all just overwhelming. This is too much to take on.

There's too much to do. It's too much to handle.

Is this your daily dialogue when thinking about your business? Did that dialogue just intensify during the pandemic? Be honest…there's no one here except for you and me.

If this is you, I want to tell you it's okay. I'm not judging. The feeling is understandable.

But here's the thing…if you're reading this book, you signed up to be in business. You wanted to be a business owner. When things are going well, you likely love being in business. You see what it creates and what it can do for you. It is not an arranged marriage. It is not something you have to do. It is not something assigned to you by someone else. It is not happening to you.

So I want to allow you to bail right now if you don't want to be in business.
If you're going to work for someone else and hang it all up, then so be it. Not everyone is cut out for this type of stuff.

However, if you are committed to being a business owner and you are committed to winning no matter what, then I need you to stop and say a huge "hell, yeah" before reading further.

Go on. I'm waiting.

(Still here? Good.)

Now let's talk about some of the harsh realities of owning a business.
Many burdens come with business. What are some of those burdens? In my case, I took on the burden of paying people. I took on the burden of having employees, and those employees took a job with me because hopefully they wanted to do the job and they are a good fit for that job, but they also took on that role with me because I was committed to paying them for a service. They depend on being paid for that service to pay their bills and take care of their families. That's a burden.

Many of you took on the burden of hiring vendors or having a virtual assistant. You took on the burden of having an accountant, an attorney—and those people depend on you for their livelihood and for the services they provide.

Many of you have taken on the burden of clients. You accepted the burden of "I'm going to work with people, and I'm going to be there for them, and I'm going to be committed to them."

And when times are tough, that's when people genuinely need you. And so you take on the burden of going the extra mile, delivering more content, more value, going above and beyond to reach out to your clients more than is necessary.

These are all examples of the kinds of burdens you take on in business. You also take on the burden of some debt and some financial risks. You commit to these burdens because you signed up for this when you became a business owner.

***Burden* is not a bad word.**
I think the word *burden* gets a bad rap. It's used way too often in the context of too heavy a responsibility for one to bear. But by definition, *burden* means "that which is carried." It is something we choose to take on (most of the time).

The critical thing to consider is that we are the ones who add emotional meaning to the word itself. We are the ones who choose to let it have a negative connotation.

The fact of the matter is that if your business has no burdens, you have no business. Business by definition implies taking risks, and taking risks means taking on responsibilities as a mechanism for growth. And with those responsibilities come problems.

And guess what…you need those problems.

YOU NEED PROBLEMS

In this "new normal" we all are experiencing, for your business to work for you, you need burdens; you need a LOT of problems if this will be a prosperous time for you.

Let me explain to you what I mean by that:

- You need people who you need to pay.
- You need people who need you.
- You need to be worried about where the money's going to come from.
- You need to have the burden of where your leads will come from and where your next client will come from.
- You need to say to yourself, "What am I going to do?"
- You need the problem of "Is there enough?"
- You need to be worried.
- You need to feel the need.

Without problems, you won't be able to do what it takes to make your business successful right now.

For those of you who have many problems right now, it means you took many risks. It means you made many decisions. It means you stepped up over and over again. And when everybody else was worried about doing this or that, you were committed to taking action, right?

So that means you need many problems to survive right now.
You also need many problems to make money right now. For the money you make, and the money you can make, and the potential money you can make, you need there to be problems right now.

Because when you have problems, you have the motivation to find solutions.

The more problems we have right now, the better you are positioned.
Right now, many of you are getting fatigued. You're getting exhausted. You're getting frustrated. And you're getting overwhelmed. And throughout the pandemic and even as the world starts to open up again, many of you are asking, "When is this going to be over? Is it ever going to end? When can I move on? This is becoming too big of a burden for me to bear."

Let me be blunt: You don't have a purpose in life without having problems.

Write that down.

You are purposeless if you are problem-less.

Put another way...you're useless if you're problem-less. No, you're not useless as a human being, but if you cannot be useful to those who need you, you are useless. And when you have problems, you become resourceful enough to find a way to resolve those problems.

This is a message that's important for everyone in your life to hear. It's something you should share with everyone in your life who's complaining about their problems:

- Your neighbor who's been worried and burdened (there's the word again) with money problems
- Your client who's a little overwhelmed right now
- Your spouse or partner who's worried about the kids
- Your team members who are feeling stressed out

Tell everyone who's complaining and let them know they are purposeless without their problems.

Without problems, you have nothing to offer.

You have nothing to do.

You have nothing to fix.

You have nothing to focus on.

You have nothing to sell.

You have nothing to innovate.

No problems mean no purpose. No problems mean no risk. No problems mean you're stuck and idle. You can't be stuck and idle in business.

Rapper Notorious B.I.G. (Biggie Smalls) had it right. "Mo Money, Mo Problems."

No problems, no money.
I woke up this morning and thought about the problems staring me in the face. They were so big, so huge, so diversified, that I said, "I am blessed. I got this. I know what to do today. I know how to put out fires. I know how to problem-solve. I know how to step up. I know how to ask people. I know how to tell people. I know how to move forward. Why? Because all of these problems mean that I've got opportunities."

Every problem is an opportunity. The moment you meet with your team or your business partner or your spouse and say, "Oh, my gosh, we're problem-free," it means you are done.

And so, I invite you to spread the gospel of problems. Your people need to know this. Your customers need to know that they have problems. They are everywhere. Most importantly, they are not a bad thing. Yes, it can seem overwhelming. It can seem daunting.

But when we attack them…

When we address them…

When we are embracing them…

All those problems are the opportunities to win.

HOW TO TURN PROBLEMS INTO MONEY

Let's say you want to make $10,000 today. To do this, you simply need ten problems to solve, each with a monetary value of $1,000.

10 problems x $1,000 a problem = $10,000.

That seems kind of simple, right? It is when you come from a place of acknowledging that many problems need to be solved, and more importantly, that others place a monetary value on solving those problems.

Find the problems. Find the opportunities. Find the money.
Your customers pay you because they have problems that they can no longer tolerate. Paying you is worth no longer dealing with whatever issue it is that they have. If they share their problem, and you present a solution that makes their lives better, then there's no way for them not to say yes.

I call it the Law of Common Sense.
Common sense tells me that Anne has an issue and she is losing her mind over it. I have a simple, affordable solution that will return her

sanity; the law of common sense says that if it's REALLY a problem for her, she will be willing to invest to solve it. If she is, then it's an actual problem. If she's not, then it isn't.

Find the ten $1,000 problems you can solve, and you can have yourself a $10,000 day.

So what are the ten problems you can solve?

Who are the people you can solve them for?

What solutions do you offer to make it incredibly easy for them to pay you to make them go away?

To be clear...I'm not suggesting you need to solve ten different problems. You may be able to solve the same problem for ten different people. The most important thing to recognize is that everyone's situation is unique.

Let's use you as an example. Think about the most significant problem you have right now. You know, the one that is:

- Costing you time
- Costing you money
- Impacting your health
- Keeping you awake at night
- Costing you your peace of mind
- Costing you your sanity

- Costing you your expertise
- Costing you your exposure

What is causing you urgent pain right now?
It might be a physical problem. It might be an event you're putting on that you're having a hard time filling. Maybe it's not enough phone clients. Perhaps it's clients who are slow to pay. Perhaps it's your damn dog who won't stop barking when you're on sales calls. Perhaps you don't have enough time to do what you want to do.

I could solve every one of those problems—except the physical problem; that one is not in my wheelhouse.

But every single other one of those problems is an easy solution.

And if I can connect with ten individuals who are feeling pain around not solving these problems, who are really serious about finding answers to these problems, and if I can present them with the solution, I will have a $10,000 day.

I assign a $1,000 value to each problem, and I say, "Would you exchange $1,000 for a solution to that problem?"

Think about it. If you knew the problem that was causing you the most urgent pain right now could be solved over the course of seven to fourteen days—or not even solved 100 percent, but even by 70 to 80 percent, would you invest $1,000? Would it be worth it to you to invest $1,000 to resolve that problem?

Some of you reading this might be saying, "Hell, yeah!" Some of you might be saying, "Well, yes ... if I had $1,000 ..."

That's a mindset issue. If you think you don't have the money to invest in what you need to invest right now, that's a massive mindset issue. *Money was everywhere during the height of the pandemic.* It's everywhere *right now.* There's more money right now than there's ever been because there are so many opportunities, opportunities that were never there before.

The solution to that mindset issue is that you must realize that you need problems.
You need to assign a value to those problems. You need your problems, and you need other people's problems. That's how you flip this whole thing on its head.

It's easier than you think. Sadly, most people make it complicated because you believe that problems are obstacles. But in reality, those problems are your only opportunity.

Problems are not in your way—they are the way.

LET ME PREACH AT YOU, SUE EVANS STYLE
Sue Evans is my momma. And my momma gives a sermon better than just about anyone else I've ever heard.

So listen up: If you genuinely have a problem, and you know that somebody could help you solve that problem, and you don't at least explore how that problem could be solved for you, you've got to ask yourself if you're even willing to do this. You've got to ask yourself if you should even be in business. Are you even willing to step up to do what you need to do to help people? You've got to ask yourself if you even want to help people. You need to ask yourself if you want to be in business. Because if you want to be in business, you would do the bare minimum to keep this thing going. Otherwise, all you're doing is making excuses so that you can fail in a socially acceptable way.

Failure is not okay.

People often say, "Fail forward."

I say, "Fuck that."

I don't want anybody failing forward.

I want you to win.

I want you to succeed.

I want you to get the clients.

I want you to get the customers.

Today is the day—not some year, not next year, not next month. Today!

Most of you reading this book are in business because you signed up to be in business. *You signed up for ALL of it, not just parts of it. You're committed, right?*

Do you know what commitment is? Commitment has nothing to do with feelings. Commitment also has nothing to do with money. When I hear somebody say, "If I only had the money . . ." I have to look at them and say, "How committed are you?"

Because there is always money for what you want.

There is always money for what you need.

Remember what I said at the start of this chapter. You signed up for business. It was not an accident. So if you signed up for it, then commitment is what it takes to grow through it, and many problems are required to make all of this work. Lots of problems are needed if you want to win no matter what.

Solving one problem gets you to the next problem and the next problem after that. Think of it as a garden pathway; you go from problem to problem to problem, and you solve each one. And each one you solve is money and success and a win. We all need problems to be successful.

So start finding ten problems today, assigning $1,000 to each problem, and then having a $10,000 day. This is not easy, but it is simple, so don't make it more complicated than it needs to be.

The bottom line is this: You need problems. Understanding this is a sophisticated thought process. When you see that problems are the way, you are in a sophisticated state of neuroscience and brain science and psychology—more than probably everyone around you. Understanding this is going to be the reason you succeed. Problems are the way to win no matter what!

CHAPTER 3

Responsive vs. Reactive

"Life is 10% what happens to you and 90% how you react to it."
-Charles R. Swindoll

In baseball, the curveball is one of the most devastating throws in a pitcher's arsenal. By its very nature, it's designed to throw you off; the ball acts in bizarre ways that make it very hard to know how to respond. Most of the time, we don't respond. We react. And that's the problem.

When life throws us a curveball, we're just like the batter; we're shocked at first. We feel thrown off and confused, and if we don't realize that everything has gone sideways, we can quickly strike out. When the pandemic hit, most of us realized that the world had changed. We knew we had to make adjustments. Sure, it was easy for a week or two…but when we started to see that things weren't going back to normal any time soon, an overwhelming sense of fatigue began to kick in.

We became tired of not being able to see our friends.

We got tired of big grocery runs and cooking every single meal.

For me, I got tired of not being able to be with people, including my clients and those whom I meet at the live events our company puts on.

Maybe you think of yourself as a steely-eyed warrior who says they can just go on interminably. But for the rest of us (me included), we can't ignore those curveballs.

When the fatigue kicks in, we have to address it. It's a part of our lives that I call "emotional business management," where we need to find ways to balance how we feel with what needs to get done.

There are two ways to handle emotional business management: We can be responsive or reactive.
For many, when you're amid this emotional fatigue, you may just want someone to tell you what to do. You want someone else in control. You want someone else making choices.

That, unfortunately, is living in a reactive state. "Tell me what to do. Show me what to do. I just don't know what I should be doing." Reactive states *feel* easier because it means you give up responsibility. It means you give up your power. It also means you are being dictated to instead of thinking. It might feel good for the moment, but ultimately it doesn't serve you.

"What should I be doing?" That is the wrong question.

When someone asks me what they should be doing (and remember, I get paid to tell people what to do), I turn it around on them and ask a different series of questions:

- What do you need?
- What is your biggest problem?
- What is your biggest pain?
- What do you feel the most urgency for getting done?"

Those are the questions that start a conversation; those are questions you can respond to. Those are the questions that get you out of panic, out of your lizard brain, and back in control.

Responsiveness is conversational.

Responsiveness allows you to engage with someone.

It's a give-and-take, not looking for someone else to be in control.

Responsiveness allows you to respond in new ways. It can spark new ideas, perhaps give you fresh content for your business. It can give you new insights into how you can support your clients and help them through whatever reactionary state they are in.

Reaction is the opposite. Reaction breaks you down to your most base reactions. Reaction constricts the imagination and makes you feel as though you are simply fighting for survival.

So when your life is turned upside down, take a step back and look at whether you are being reactionary or responsive.
One way to tell is to look at the state of your business. Are you having conversations? Are you reaching out? Are you talking to people? Are you active on social media? If you're not, it's a sure sign you are in reactive mode.

Reactionary is all about you.

Responsiveness is taking the focus off of yourself.

When someone asks you what you need, you can think. You can create content. It's excellent coaching. It's excellent consulting. It's supporting others, and it enables you to have a high-level, intelligent conversation.

HOW TO GET INTO A RESPONSIVE STATE

A moment of honesty: Have you been in a reactive state? It's okay if you have. The first step toward getting out of it is realizing you've been in that place. There's no need to feel bad or berate yourself. Simply say, "I'm done with this shit. Let's move on." Good. Great.

Now it's time to simply ask yourself, what do I know I need to do today?

That may be a challenging question for you.

It may be scary for you.

It may be hard for you.

It may be fearsome for you.

It may be uncomfortable for you.

It may be unusual for you.

I get it. But if you only did one thing today that you knew would move you forward, even a little, what would it be?

Remember, systems and ideas and innovation are not for the good times. They're for the bad times. You prepare during the good times, so when the bad times come along, you're ready.

So what is that one thing? Write it down. Put it where you can see it. Act on it.

Look at what you wrote and say to yourself: "If I need to do it today, I needed to do it yesterday, and I need to do it tomorrow."

If you're doing this right, it's monotonous.

If you are doing this right, it's boring.

If you are doing this right, it's exhausting.

If you're doing this right, it's like the same thing over and over and over and over again.

Get over it.

It's in that monotony, in that consistency, in that boredom, that you get the most results.

It's in that boring, repetitive place that the winning happens.

That doesn't sound very sexy, does it?

It doesn't sound like a very persuasive marketing tool.

But the hard reality is this: If you're doing this right, it should feel boring because you're doing the same thing over and over in a consistent way.

By doing the same thing you know you need to do today, tomorrow, and the next day, you're going to start to build consistency.

Consistency builds traction.

Traction builds action.

Action builds results.

Inaction leads to nothing.

Inaction leads to stagnation.

Every day of waiting and uncertainty you allow yourself to fall into is another day of lost revenue.
It's another day of lost challenges. So I'm here to tell you that you have to keep going. You have to do it smartly; you have to do it healthily. Because every day you get behind means that you are going to be behind for months.

When things look bleak, you can choose to rally, and you need to be rallying for your business. You need to be rallying for your clients. You need to be rallying for your family. You don't want to be the kind of business owner who sits there, wringing your hands and saying, "Oh my God; what do we do now? What do we do now? Because this is so hard."

News flash: It's *always* been hard; you just didn't have an excuse for it being hard. Now you do.

The difference between responsiveness and reactionary is one of choice. You can choose to meet the challenges you face, to stay active, to stay engaged…or you can fold. It's that simple. Because the reality is that responsiveness is nothing more than a delaying tactic.

It's time to remember that you have a skill or talent, something that you were born with or developed, and you are using that to build a business. The choice to be responsive is your choice. It's about following what you know, and it's knowing that you know more than you think you do. You've rehearsed, studied, and planned. You've practiced again and again and mastered your skillset.

And when times are tough, you should rely on what you already know. You should trust your muscle memory. That's how you win, even when things are scary.

AN EXAMPLE OF RESPONSIVENESS IN ACTION

I love boating. I love being out on the water. But when boating, it is imperative to understand your buoy markers and shore markings. When I bought my first boat years ago, I really didn't know how much I needed to learn about safely navigating the waters.

I tended to take the same route every time I went out in my new boat, which was almost daily. I knew that route by heart.

But what if I took a different route?

What if circumstances changed, and I found myself out in my boat at night, without the security of daylight?

How would I know where to go then?

One beautiful summer night in Maine, I had the opportunity to find out. We got caught out in the boat late at night and had to use a flashlight to navigate around lobster buoys and dry land.

I freaked The. Fuck. Out. I was trying to remain calm, but I was terrified. It was like the water had somehow dropped us on some other planet. My heart was racing, and my anxiety level was through the roof. It was the same route I had taken many times during the day, but now it was as if I had never taken that path and had no clue what to do next. The land looked like water, and the water looked like land. Where the hell was I?

Fortunately, we eventually managed to find our way. Once I had navigated myself back to land successfully, I made the business connection. This is what happens to so many entrepreneurs. When circumstances change, we forget everything we ever knew. We behave just like all the other times we have traveled our business paths, but now the landscape has changed, and it no longer works.

We are in the dark. We can't find our way. And we start to panic.

We have to learn how to navigate through uncharted territory. In these times, it means taking advantage of new opportunities to connect, new opportunities to act and create new paths for your business to thrive. While everyone else around you is slowing down, panicking because the world has changed, you can slide right in and take advantage of all the missed opportunities.

While others are hanging back and feeling paralyzed, you can book yourself solid.

Step into responsiveness and step out of reaction.
It's one of the greatest lessons you can learn during times of upheaval and uncertainty because then, no matter what life throws at you, you'll respond from a place of strength rather than react from a place of weakness.

CHAPTER 4

Showing Up No Matter What

At times, I feel like a broken record. For almost twelve years, I've been telling my clients, Facebook followers, and anyone within a fifteen-mile radius who will listen to me that businesses don't close because they run out of money; they close because they run out of ideas.

In our last chapter, we talked about how operating from a reactive state can cause you to run out of ideas, abdicate your thought process, and leave you feeling stuck. So now I want to spend some time reinforcing that half of what makes our company so successful isn't just that we are brilliant at what we do (which I think we are, naturally), but because we show up every day, no matter what is going on.

Staying Disciplined

When the pandemic of 2020 hit, my team started to work from home. We were committed to staying isolated and helping one another to keep safe. I'll be the first to admit that having my team work remotely wasn't easy for me. I thrive on the energy of being in person, and I believe that being physically present with my team allows us to stay in the right mindset of our company's goals.

I remember telling my team that staying on point while working from home, and with all the chaos coming at us from the news, our family members, and community, would require discipline—not the discipline of doing what our job entails but rather the discipline to think the way we're supposed to think. I cautioned my team about falling into a reactive state. I empowered them to be responsive, to stay focused, and not just forget everything they already knew.

Above anything else, I reminded them that we had to keep showing up and, more importantly, stay disciplined.

The worst decision you can make in the middle of a crisis is to blow up everything you have been doing, to go, "Oh no. I'm not going to move forward," or "I'm not going to do this," or "I'm going to stop." The worst decision you could make is to do nothing and wait.

When times are tough, my team doesn't put anything on hold.

We're not "waiting and seeing" on anything. Obviously, we've had to shift some things during the 2020 pandemic. We started working from home. Our masterminds went virtual. We even held a virtual event!

But the one thing we refused to do was put the brakes on the things that run our business and our livelihood.

So keep going. Keep running your business. Double down; reach out to people. Don't throw away your business.

Don't throw away your business model.

Don't throw away the opportunities that you have in front of you.

Do, however, be observant enough that we may require specific shifts.

Do realize that the way you service your clients and customers may deviate from what it has been.

Do remember that your clients need you now more than ever.

Our world will be normal again. Hell, by the time you're reading this, things may have turned back to "normal." The world is going to continue to run and exist and be present. Business is going to happen, and money is going to be exchanged.

The question is: Are you going to be prepared for it, or are you going to be behind the eight ball because you stopped, waited, and fretted?

It's understandable—we're all guilty of doing a little fretting these days. But I see so much of this fretting; I'm seeing so many people panicking and standing still and waiting—and that is a crisis in itself.

Things might feel out of control and icky and rough and uncertain and scary, even horrifying at times, but remember, as Mary Morrissey says, "Hold the vision, not the circumstance."

Because remember, this is not the last crisis you will face in your lifetime or your business. Hopefully, it won't be on the same global scale as we have just encountered, but it can come in many forms: The laws surrounding your industry can change, a loved one may get sick or die, or one of a hundred other things can happen. The point is not to focus on what may go wrong but to remember that there will always be something hiding around the corner you haven't prepared for, which is all the more reason you need to stay focused.

WHAT IF THERE'S NO UNDERSTUDY?

Recently I came down with a cold. I thought it was just allergies, but then it turned into a full-blown cold. On top of that, I had dental work done. I've hardly ever needed dental work. I had my first cavity filled when I was twenty-eight years old. I only have two cavities, but one was filled improperly and turned into something crazy. I needed a root canal. That turned into needing a crown. So my head was full and stuffed, and my mouth was swollen too. This got me thinking about the question: What do you do when you have to keep going, and there's no one to take over?

I always tell parents, "Put your kids in theater, because if there's one thing that you can learn really, really well from theater, it is that usually there are no understudies. As a kid, I did lots of theater, and I learned this lesson more than once. I remember not feeling my best but still having to go on—just having to show up and do it. And I remember as a kid going, "I'm tired." But I was in a show, and people had bought tickets, and I had to do it.

I love what theater taught me about showing up no matter what. And in business, it's very similar. Many of us are solopreneurs. If you're sick and also your vendors' primary support team, you can undoubtedly have a sick day, but if it's the day of their big launch and you're supposed to push all the buttons to make it happen, what are you going to do?

I'm now in my eleventh year of doing events. I've done hundreds and hundreds of events at this point, and I have been sick as a dog at times. One time I even had a cardiac incident on the night before my big pitch; the doctors had to restart my heart. Sometimes I've been fortunate to have had a partner in crime or some team members who could pinch-hit for me. I could have some people take a little bit of the burden off me, so I didn't have to be on stage as much. But I've also had moments where it was just me, and I had to figure out what to do. I had to figure out how to do it. I've learned that you need to think about a few things when you're trying to figure out how to keep going when you're a solo machine, but you really, truly need to take time off.

When that happens, you have to be prepared to answer the following questions:

How can you have everything systematized and organized?

How can you not feel guilty about taking care of yourself?

And most importantly, how do you not lose money when you do it?

For me, first and foremost, I really do have a "keep going" mindset. I have a "keep going" attitude. So just because I had a cold and a swollen mouth, I didn't cancel calls. I didn't cancel meetings. I respected the fact that I had people who have been waiting for weeks to have a call with me. I recognized that things could be worse. Sure, I might take a few breaks in between everything, but I keep going and stay in the game.

Now, there are times when you absolutely, positively have to stop. There are times when nothing will help unless you go into your room, close the door, turn your phone off, put your head under the covers, and just rest something out.

The question at hand isn't if this will happen, but when. When you need one of those days, that's when I highly suggest that you have a system in place. No, I'm telling you: You must have a plan in place. Without a system in place, I couldn't disappear for a day without my business shutting down. Without deadlines being missed or goals not being reached. Without a plan in place, I would genuinely be a lead actress with no understudy.

That's why you don't want to be a one-person or one-woman band. I want you to have some kind of support, even if initially it's just very light support. And I want you to have your systems in place to the point where you could have a five-minute conversation with some-body, and they could pick up exactly where you were. They could jump in, support you, and take over what you were doing.

I know that at times I give the impression that I never stop. But there are times when I do need to take a day. But when I do, I never do that without some type of backup. This is true even if I have client calls that I've had to cancel because of a family emergency or I've been so sick that I couldn't lift my head off of the pillow. During those instances, I've always said, "I need to reschedule, but would you want to talk to one of my other coaches? Do you have something on your plate you really need to speak to somebody about? Do you want to jump in and talk to a team member?"

So do you have a backup for you?
Do you have an understudy? Do you have someone who can step in when you can't so that your business can keep going without you?

GET GRITTY
Showing up no matter what is easier when you develop grit. *Grit* is defined as "firmness of mind or spirit; unyielding courage in the face-off hardship or danger."

Developing grit begins with learning that you cannot go jump in bed and hide for three days every time you get a sniffle. It's real-izing that every time a call doesn't go your way, you don't raise the white flag and threaten to walk off the court. It means being able to honestly assess when a situation requires you to step away and when to power through. Developing grit means learning tenacity and some level of endurance. I genuinely believe that those who win are not always the smartest or most talented, but those who have the most grit and perseverance. They are the ones who stay in the game no matter what. They make phone calls when they don't feel well. They show up and write when they don't feel inspired. They follow through on what they said they would because that's who they are. They're able to be a leader and get on stage even in an inopportune time.

This also applies to life events.

Five days before my very first event started, my partner Melonie's father went into hospice. I remember sleeping on the floor of his room for several days. When he passed away, I left Melonie and went to my event. She had to stay for his funeral and flew in a day later. And while every fiber in my being wanted to stay with her during this time, we both knew that 165 people were flying in from all over the world. I had team members there. I had speakers lined up to speak. I was committed, and those people depended on me. Now, those people are lovely, compassionate people who would have been very generous and understanding if we had told them what was going on. But the truth of the matter is they don't care what's going on with me. They were coming to my event because they had business problems and issues, and they needed help. So, the bottom line was that I had to show up and shine because I committed to doing that. It wasn't easy. Was I at my best 100 percent of the time? No, I'm not sure that

I was, but I was probably at 80 to 85 percent, and that's pretty damn good for most people.

What are you made of?

When something happens, do you see it as an obstacle you need to problem-solve and strategize around, or do you throw up your hands and say, "I'd better crawl back in bed"? When shit goes sideways, do you tell yourself, "I better just quit," or "I better just cancel"? Do you rely on the understanding of others to make it okay for you not to follow through?

There's a reason that I went from kindergarten to twelfth grade and never missed a day of school. *My parents instilled in me that going to school was my job.* It was the one thing that I had to do. And even if I didn't show up every day 100 percent, I still had to show up.

Even if I didn't feel like going, I still had to go.

Even if I didn't feel well, it was my job to go.

Even if a teacher was mean to me, staying home wasn't an option.

I also knew that if I went there and didn't feel like I could make it through the day, my parents would get me, and I'd go home. But I also knew it was my obligation to do what I was supposed to do. And what I was supposed to do was go to school. This left such a mark on me for the rest of my life that sometimes I have guilt if I do need to miss something or I really can't do something. I'll find myself thinking, "Oh my God, my parents would tell me to go to school. My parents would tell me to go to school." But truthfully, that's rare. I like to fulfill my obligations. I always feel bad when I can't meet an obligation.

You have to learn the difference between knowing when you have to say no to an obligation and saying no because you just don't feel like doing it.
You've got to dig in and figure out how resilient you are. How gritty you are.

It's time to ask yourself:

Do you have the endurance that it takes to keep showing up no matter what?

To keep showing up when you're not at your best?

To keep showing up when the strategy fails? To keep showing up when your nose is stuffed up?

To keep showing up when you get the stomach flu?

To keep showing up when you and your spouse get in a huge fight?

To keep showing up when your child has an issue that you need to address or deal with?

I can't tell you how many times I get on the phone with people, and they say, "Well, I haven't really been working my business for a month because X, Y, or Z happened."

I just don't have that luxury. I have a business that needs to feed me. It needs to feed my son; it needs to feed my family. And it needs to feed eighteen full-time employees. It needs to fulfill clients who have paid us and who we are obligated to take care of.

So, do not be that person who, when something happens, you shut down.

Do not be that person who thinks it's easier to stop than it is to push through.

Instead, be that person who has some damn common sense and can figure out how to rest when you need to. Who has a plan in place for when shit goes down? Be the person who says, "I am gritty enough to get through this."

Melonie's mother was sick for many, many, many years with lung disease, and she was on oxygen for as long as I've been with Melonie, which is twenty-five years. She always wore makeup, at least 85 percent of the time. And the more makeup she had on, the worse we knew she felt. She would always say, "Guys, when there are things out of your control, control the things you can. I may not feel good today, but I can look good, and I can show up in the best way I can."

You may not feel perfect today. Something may be going on in your life. Maybe you have the sniffles as I do. Maybe you hurt your back. Maybe somebody hurt your feelings. But can you show up and be gritty today? Can you show up today and endure? The mind will stop before the body needs to, so keep going. And then when you can't keep going, no one will be annoyed. Those who are annoying are the ones who always seem sick; they always seem crazy. They always seem like they have something going on. They always have to cancel.

People don't feel that way about me because they know if I'm down for the count, I am genuinely down for the count and something is wrong. That way, you don't become a "cry wolf" kind of person. So get gritty today and keep going.

CHAPTER 5

The Just Say No Scam

I'm going to hopefully dig into something that I know some of you will have opinions about.

Some of you will agree with what I'm about to say.

Some of you will disagree.

Some will fall somewhere in the middle.

Before I make my statement, I want to explain why I'm doing it: I want to challenge some of your thoughts about your business. When we challenge our thoughts, we challenge the actions that we take. And when we challenge the actions we take, we challenge the way we work and the energy we put into our work.

Because ultimately, you're reading this book because you want to win and because you care about profitability.

Preamble done.

Here's what I want to share: You are being manipulated.

You are being manipulated by the media.

You are being manipulated in the personal development space.

You are being manipulated in the coaching space.

A scam is manipulating you. I call it "The Just Say No Scam."

First, I think we can all agree that most of you want to make more money. Can I get a "yes" to that? Great. So if you want to make more money, then that means you have to show up in a certain way. You have to take specific actions every day, regardless of how you feel, to reach your goals.

Now, there has been a trend in the last couple of years around vulnerability, and boundaries, and "the power of saying no." It's this trend of just walking away, cutting ties, and ending things you don't like so you can take control of your life, which means you can just turn something off, create new boundaries, cut something off, and you need to do that to be healthy. You need to say no so that you can say yes to everything else.

A point of delineation:

There is a kernel in there that is true and useful.

There is a kernel in there that is a scam.

The scam part is hurting your life; it is hurting your profitability, hurting you. That scam? The permission to stop. The permission to quit. The permission to simply walk away.

This is heavy, so take a deep breath because I want you to ground yourself in honesty. I want you to ground yourself in truth right now. I want you to ground yourself in being the best self-coach you have ever been to yourself.

Now I want you to ask yourself in the last year, what have you stopped, quit, or ended, as it related to your business or personal growth?
This should be something that you convinced yourself that it was socially acceptable to stop doing. Something you coached yourself into being okay around stopping. Something you told yourself it made sense to stop doing because of, you know, reasons.

Most importantly—it should be something that wasn't necessary for you to stop, quit, or end.

Now let me be very clear here. I'm not talking about abusive relationships or things that put you in danger or something that put your family, your life, or your business in danger. I'm also aware that if there is one thing the pandemic did for many people, it helped them evaluate what was truly important to them and what they wanted to focus their life, time, and energy on.

This is not what I am speaking about.

I'm talking about your work.

I'm talking about your business.

I'm talking about your health. I'm talking about things that you knew were on some level for the betterment of you.

But they were hard or challenging, or maybe they got annoying, or the person who was leading you through those was bossy or pushy, or you weren't in alignment with them. Right? You told yourself it wasn't worth the effort. So, under the guise of vulnerability, you started saying no and creating boundaries because it was socially acceptable not to have to do the things you didn't want to or be around someone who doesn't always make you feel good.

This is the manipulation. This is the scam. The confusion between saying no to the things that could physically hurt your spirit or health and those that can damage your business because they are annoying.

YOU WILL HAVE TO SAY YES MORE THAN YOU SAY NO

The bottom line is that if you want to make more money, you will need to say yes more than you say no. You will need to say yes to investments that will help your business grow. You will need to say yes to opportunities that will stretch your comfort level on the path to getting you where you want to end up.

Some of the yeses will be challenging.

Some of the yeses will be ugly.

Some of the yeses will be beautiful.

Some of the yeses will be amazing.

Some will be disasters.

But to move forward, you need to say yes more than you say no.

Don't fall victim to the vulnerability vultures.
Too many of us are listening to the internet evangelists and lifestyle gurus who tell you that you need to be more vulnerable and more protective of yourself at the expense of your ability to make money. Too many of us are buying into the premise of saying more boundaries will protect you. Quitting will help you move forward. It's okay if you are six feet from gold—you have permission not to do the hard stuff. You have permission because you simply don't feel like it to walk away. And it's cool.

It's not fucking cool. I want you to be honest with yourself right now because the only way we get better results, bigger results, more profits is when we are brutally honest with ourselves. When we're brutally truthful with ourselves and don't let ourselves get away with stuff, right?

Boundaries are essential to a certain level. But most people put up bullshit boundaries.
This is the manipulation and the confusion that I'm talking about. People say, "I can't be around those people. I can't be in this environment. I can't put myself in a situation that makes me feel uncomfortable."

Do you know how many people that I'm around that I don't love being with? How many people I am around who I don't even like? I might not like them, but I'm smart and evolved enough to know I have something to learn from them. Putting up a boundary only prevents me from learning. I can be around people if there's something to gain. I can experience people even if I don't love every moment of the interaction. I don't have to put up fences and walls and boundaries; I still get good even when there's bad. Right?

So sure, we all need *some* boundaries. Sure, we need to say no to *some* things. But we have become a culture of extreme boundaries and evangelizing, saying no, stopping, and making it okay to quit. We've gotten so focused on coddling our egos and giving each other pats on the back just for participating.

There are no participation trophies in entrepreneurship.
There is only a first, second, or third place. And if you're second or third place, it means you are one or two places behind first. That is just the way it works.

And that's the difference between the amateurs and the pros.

HONORING YOUR FEELINGS

Let me be 100 percent transparent and honest. If I were honoring my feelings every day, I'd be upstairs watching Netflix. I'd be hanging out with my son, Adrien, and eating seven course tasting menus in Paris every single day, twenty-four hours a day. If all I did was honor how I was feeling, I wouldn't get anything done that gets me the life I have.

If you are spending all your time honoring how you're feeling, you are not getting the life you want either. The truth is that our feelings are tricky. They tell us things aren't fair. They tell us that because it's hard, it's not good for you. If it creates anxiety or stress, or worry, or concern, you should stop.

Feelings are tricky. They are gremlins, and the gremlin's job is to make you feel good. So your feelings will lie to you and cheat; they will prod and poke and nag because they just want you to feel good. They don't hold the vision for the goals you have—they hold the vision for feeling good at that moment.

Because the reality is that when you say yes to the things that will help you achieve your goals, you will get the rewards you want. When you say yes to the hard things—the things that help you build consistency when you create a plan and follow-through, regardless if you're sick, hungry, or tired, you create the results you want and the life you envision.

And you know what? That *feels* really fucking good.

CHAPTER 6

Becoming Positively Dangerous

"The most dangerous person is the one who listens, thinks, and observes."
–Bruce Lee

I want to let you in on a little secret I think you're going to like: You are about to become positively dangerous.

I'm serious.

Take that in a minute.

Positively. Dangerous.

And this isn't just a good thing. It's a fucking amazing thing.

Check this out: Psychological research has shown for decades that people who are positive and resilient throughout a crisis come out on the other side of it as a dangerous weapon for getting whatever they want, doing whatever they need to do, and living the life of their dreams.

There's more: People who have been through massive natural disasters such as forest fires or horrible hurricanes, or those who have had a tragic death in their family, as so many have experienced through the coronavirus pandemic—often these are the people who can create good from these events. They are the ones who can do good from it. Why? Because they were resilient through it.

And they are the very people who become positive weapons for change. Suddenly, they realize they can do anything. They know they can get through anything.

If you develop resiliency through the tough times, you will become someone who plays to win.
You become someone who does what you need to. You don't stop. You don't lie down. You don't let whatever the current crisis is get the best of you. You don't listen to all the bullshit negative news.

If you are committed to finding the good, taking the right action, and never giving up, on the other side of this, you will become so dangerous in a positive way that no one will know what to do.

You will be unstoppable. You will do everything that you are called to do. Every time you hit a roadblock, you will just close your eyes and bust through it. Whenever something doesn't go your way, you won't care because you know there's another way. You have become dangerous.

Let others choose to become followers.

Let others just kind of get through things.

You are someone who is about to become a dangerous weapon for good. You will boldly say there will not be people left behind.

There will not be hungry kids.

There will not be a shitty education system.

There will not be people who cannot find what they need to see in the world academically.

There will be education for everyone.

There will not be people who are struggling to pay their electricity bills.

There will not be an environment that is falling apart.

There will not be any of this because you will be a dangerous weapon for good. You will be dangerous because you will know you can get through anything. You can make anything happen—because if you can make it through the shit sandwich of a global pandemic, then you can get through any other thing that comes your way.

This isn't the science of Suzanne. To repeat: Therapeutic research shows that resilient people, people who know they will come out on the other side of a crisis, these people take the hits and they take the licks, and they get up and they keep going.

What's even better? As they keep going, they pull other people with them.

They help other people; they lead other people—and when the crisis is entirely over, they become the leaders of the world.

When you come from a place of resilience, you become a self-led person who goes, "It doesn't matter that this didn't work. It doesn't matter that this broke. It doesn't matter that this has happened to me because I can get through anything."

Let me give you a news flash: You have a 100 percent track record of getting through bad things.

You're still here.

You're showing up.

You're ready to learn.

You're serving clients.

You're helping customers.

You're getting new customers.

You're still breathing.

You have a 100 percent perfect, positive track record of getting through hard things.

Stop and say out loud: "I can get through anything."

Back in high school, we all had to put a quote in the yearbook, and I wrote, "With God, all things are possible." I knew then, and I know now, I can get through anything. And so can you.

You're not only going to get through this; you're going to come out stronger on the other side of this.

When you're dangerous, no one can stop you.
Your negative neighbor cannot stop you.

Your family member telling you that you should just give up your business can't stop you.

That naysayer client who says, "You shouldn't be charging me right now," can't stop you.

The government can't stop you, and COVID-19 didn't stop you either.

You cannot be stopped because you have powerful weapons of positivity on your side.

You have God on your side.

You have your talents on your side.

You have your experience on your side.

You have your skillset on your side.

You have everything you need to be successful, to be helpful in this world right now.

You have everything you need to be profitable, be positive, lead others, support others, and make a big difference.

You have all of that on your side.

Write this down: "I've got everything I need on my side."
Say it out loud when you wake up.

Say it when you feel challenged.

Say it when you hit a home run.

A WEAPON FOR POSITIVE CHANGE
What you do today makes you a weapon tomorrow.

The ability to be resilient today makes you more dangerous tomorrow.

And that resilience will echo beyond just your lifetime. It will echo for three lifetimes because when you are resilient, you teach your children to be resilient, and they teach their children to be resilient. By becoming positively dangerous, you break the curse of generations before you that were victims and made things seem so hard. You can take part in creating an entire generation underneath you and underneath them—that creates a legacy of resilience because you are getting through this with positivity and faith.

When times are tough, I am tougher.
Do you understand the idea of calloused hands?

My dad is a farmer. I'm from a seventh-generation farm family. My dad's hands would get so calloused from moving irrigation systems and having to cut down trees and grow tobacco and work on farm equipment.

When your hands get calloused, the job gets easier.

And with all that is happening right now in the world, your hands are becoming calloused. And with every callous you get, this job gets easier. Everything you do becomes simpler. It all seems to take less effort.

When you develop calluses, it doesn't hurt as much. It doesn't sting as much. It's not as confusing. It's not as off-putting. It's not as shocking. And so, as your hands get calloused, the work gets easier. This is good because the reality is that there are more challenging times ahead. When one crisis is over, you'll be hit with the next thing. When that's over, you'll be hit with the next. Life is always throwing something at us, but what you have that you've never had before is the understanding that you can do anything. You can keep going. You are resilient; you are gifted. You are talented, your work matters, your life matters, your life experience matters.

And all we're doing is developing calloused hands so that the work gets easier. It gets easier. Life has always been hard. You're just getting tougher. You are developing calloused hands so you can do the work. What you do today makes you a weapon for tomorrow. You are dangerous!

CHAPTER 7

Who Are You in the Middle of the Night?

I have a client who is a lovely, amazing woman. She is intelligent, talented, and capable and told us that she decided to do some work with us.

Great. Awesome. Groovy. She made a decision.

But then, her doubts set in. She began to waiver. She realized that investing in herself was scary. Saying yes to herself was scary. Saying yes to using credit or her funds was scary. Choosing to have a business and asking for support can be scary.

Now, when I invest—and I spend hundreds of thousands of dollars on myself, on my consultants, on my coaching, on different vendors I use—I'm not investing in what I think I should invest in. I'm not investing in what I believe I can do or what I can get back. I'm investing the amount to which I want to get. I'm investing the amount that I believe in myself that I want to get in return.

Some of you might be agreeing with this right now, while others of you might be going, "Oh shit." I get it; it's a lot to take in. But I want you to sit and think about this for a moment. If you're too afraid to take on debt, if you're too afraid to spend money, if you're too afraid to take on risk, you have to ask yourself, "Is my business just a nice idea, or is this something I am driven and committed to doing?"

Well, this client of mine was wavering. She reached out to us and told us she wasn't sure she could do it; she thought she might have to cancel. I shared with her why this is normal. I helped her to see what she's experiencing. I shared with her what she has to do to get to where she says she wants to get. And I got her into a good place.

But then I get another email from her.

And this email is longer. A little more dramatic. It begins with, "I'm writing this in the middle of the night. I am so anxious and worried about being able to pay for this and being able to make money in my business to take care of this investment, and I'm so worried about debt."

Why am I sharing this with you?

Because it's an aha moment: You are who you truly are in the middle of the night.

You see, I also was up in the middle of the night. I was sending follow-up texts and emails to potential clients on the West Coast, responding to a couple of potential opportunities. My "middle of the night" was income-producing, and her "middle of the night" was anxiety-producing.

So my question to you is: Who are you in the middle of the night?

What actions are you taking today, yesterday, tomorrow that are potential-filled, positive-filled, making a difference-filled?

Who are you in the middle of the night?

Because who you are in the middle of the night is exactly how you show up in the middle of the day.

During the day, you can put on makeup, you can get dressed up, you can smile and put pretty Facebook posts out there. But you cannot hide who you are in the middle of the night. As Cathy Wagner, who was a client of mine for many years, said, "The night makes cowards of us all. So when nightfall comes, we really become our true selves."

What about you?

Are you waiting?

Are you avoiding?

Are you creating anxiety for yourself?

Are you creating guilt for yourself?

Are you creating shame for yourself?

Or are you creating opportunities?

Every moment can either be anxiety-producing or revenue-producing.

Every moment can build resilience. Which are you choosing? You cannot hide in the middle of the day who you are in the middle of the night. If you are full of anxiety, and delaying, and waiting, and in denial in the middle of the night, then you are half-assed, half-baked, half-worthy showing up in the middle of the day.

You have a choice every moment in your life.

You have a choice to suffer, or you have a choice to succeed.

You have a choice to build anxiety or build resilience.

If you are having middle-of-the-night wavering moments, full of uncertainty, full of not believing in yourself and not thinking you can do it, those are what you will bring to the middle of the day. So you've got to figure out your middle of the night.

WHAT'S YOUR FOCUS?
Are you fear-focused, unfocused, or strategy-focused?

The fear-focused person says, "I am not enough. I'm not taking action. I don't know enough. I'm worried that I may not get this right. I'm worried that there may not be enough."

The unfocused person says, "I'm taking some downtime. During this time, I'm going to reevaluate, and I'm going to refocus, and I'm going to reconsider what's important to me and what I need to be doing." The unfocused person also could be in denial. "I'm just going to hope this gets better. I'm going to see what happens." The unfocused person might be the person that thinks this entire thing we're going through is blown out of proportion and isn't as bad as everyone thinks it is.

The strategy-focused person is the person who has shifted their offers and their business and what they were doing within 2.4 days of a crisis happening. They are four times more likely to make changes to their team as needed. They are 5.2 times more likely to be optimistic. And they only experience 21 percent of revenue issues, whereas the fear-focused people saw a 35 percent drop in revenue.

But here's what's interesting—the unfocused person saw a 56 percent drop in revenue. It is more dangerous to be unfocused than it is to be fear-focused.

It's all about choice. You can choose to be anxiety-producing, or you can choose to be revenue-generating. It's not about being scared. It's about choosing to let the fear be anxiety-producing. We can't stop being afraid. The fear comes on; we're afraid of things. I'm afraid of snakes. I don't want to put my hand in a basket for fear there's a snake in it. That's not going to change. And it's a good thing that doesn't change because fear can protect us.

But I can choose to have the fear stop me, and that will create anxiety.

Because here's the deal: The anxiety you're having in the night, the overwhelm you're feeling in the night, all of that, all that wavering that you're having in the middle of the night—it isn't from fear. It's from not deciding. You are not having anxiety because you're afraid. You're having anxiety because you won't make the decision not to let the fear lead you. You've got to make decisions *with* fear. You've got to make decisions *through* fear. You have to make decisions in the middle of fear, standing waist-deep in fear. The fear will not go away and neither will the choice that you get to make of whether you are revenue-producing or anxiety-producing.

So who are you in the middle of the night? Because that's precisely who you bring to the middle of the day.

CHAPTER 8

Stop Watering Dead Plants

*"Don't judge each day by the harvest you reap, but by
the seeds that you plant."*
– Robert Louis Stevenson

This is a chapter that, in some ways, doesn't feel like...me. Because I'm going to be talking about plants. I'll be honest. I've got a brown thumb. Plants die around me. We have beautiful plants and flowers around my house, but it ain't got to do with my taking care of them.

The painfully obvious thing to recognize about most plants is that they grow when you take care of them. And when you don't, they die. And the funny thing about a dead plant is that once it's dead, it's dead, so there's no bringing it back (trust me, I've tried).

All of this is to say that the idea of watering dead plants is a metaphor for how so many business owners I know spend their time trying to water dead plants—putting energy, attention, money, and time into efforts, ideas, activities, and even people, all of which have no hope of growing despite their best attention. I'm not talking about plants that are hurting, withering, and with some love and attention, can be brought back from the brink and can thrive. I'm talking about the plants that we know in our hearts have no hope, yet we continue to put our time and energy into them.

What dead plants do you need to stop watering?
Here's a list of some:

The Dead Plant of Comparison

Many of us go on social media and look at that person who *seems* to be everything we wish we could be. We look at them and get lost in their beauty. We feel inferior as we tell ourselves how easy it is for them. "Look how smoothly she does it. Look how graceful she is. Look how people flock to her. I'm not as pretty. I'm not as fit. I'm not as smart. I'll never make as much money. I'll never be this accomplished." And we just keep watering this damn plant of comparison, hoping that somehow it will help us feel better when all it does is make us feel shitty.

(Side note: 95 percent of the stuff you see on social media is bullshit. People only show the good stuff and hide everything else. If you had a real insight into what goes behind the scenes of everyone you secretly compare yourself to, you'd feel a hell of a lot better about your life.)

The Dead Plant of Approval

This is an ugly one because we are all guilty of it. It's the decision to wake up each day and, consciously or subconsciously, think to ourselves, "I wonder how this person will like this choice I made.

I wonder how my parents will feel about this. I wonder what my partner will feel about this decision. Will they like it? Will they like me? Will they think I'm good? Will they agree with what I say? Will they connect with me? Will they buy from me?"

If that's you, every day, you're waking up and watering this dead plant of approval.

So many of us have a deep-seated need to be liked (and look, I want to be liked too, but I can't operate a business worrying whether or not every single person I interact with approves of what I say or do, even my partner, Melonie). It's this constant, exhausting thought process of "See me. Like me. Agree with me. Need me. Love me. Like me. Love me. Like me." It's not rational. We know we can't make everyone happy. We know we can't please everyone. If you are making everyone happy, your business is taking the wrong approach. But we continue to water this dead plant of approval, and then we wonder, "Why am I not further? Why don't I have more? Why can't I be more? Why can't I achieve more?"

And so you can continue to pour water into this plant that can ever grow, and time keeps passing you by.

How many of you have been waiting on that person, that family member, that friend, that spouse, that mentor, that boss, or that coach to tell you, "It's okay. I love you, I see you, and you're doing great"? How many of you are waiting on someone else to give you approval? To provide you with permission? That dead plant of validation. That dead plant that is never going to be your path, or your answer, or your way, or your ability to do more and be more and have more in life and business.

The Dead Plant of Wrong Clients and Customers

How many of you are investing in clients that aren't ideal for you? They are not the customers that are going to spread good words about you. They are not the clients and customers who will lift you up and send referrals, praise you, appreciate you, and acknowledge that working with you is an amazing return on their investment. They aren't even going to let you do your best work because they are more concerned with validating their assumptions than letting you do the work they hired you for. How many of you are going to keep watering those dead plants of the wrong clients and customers?

This dead plant is tricky because it's easy to tell yourself that while you do have some wrong clients, they are a necessary evil to keep the lights on. Therefore, you have to take the wrong ones while you are in the process of finding the right ones. I'm going to say this is bullshit. Sadly, every time you take the wrong client (even if it's a temporary infusion of cash to get you over the hump), you'll likely find yourself spending more and more time cultivating this dying plant, which is time that could be better spent finding a better client. And it's all the more reason you need to have your shit together and a plan in place to consistently be finding those right clients, the plants that will grow and bear fruit.

The Dead Plant of the Past

How about the past? How many of you are still watering that dead, withered plant?

Think about that for a moment.

How many of you have experienced trauma, an act of aggression against you, an act of intolerance or abuse or harassment?

How many of you have experienced in your past something that feels unforgivable?

How often do you flashback to it, think about it, ponder it?

How many of you have an experience, or a person, or a situation, or something that happened in your life that was so hurtful, so ugly, so painful, so cruel, so mean, so irrational that you can't let it go?

I think we can all relate to this one.

But. We. Have. To. Stop. Watering. That. Dead. Plant.

We've got to stop watering being ignored.

We've got to stop watering that ex-spouse.

We've got to stop watering being invisible.

We've got to stop watering being told we're not enough.

We've got to stop watering living in the past because it prevents us from moving into our future.

Michael Beckwith, a spiritual teacher and an amazing human being, said, "Forgiveness is letting go of the hope that the past could have been any different." Every time I share that or say it out loud, I get teary because there is so much freedom in that statement.

You don't have to keep dragging heavy buckets of water to this dead garden. You can just let it go. You can walk away from it. You can let the land replenish itself and heal itself because forgiveness is letting go of the hope that the past could have been any different.

Watering the dead plant in hopes the past could have been any different keeps you from making the money you should make. It's keeping you from working with the right people. It's keeping you from feeling better. It's keeping you from being better. It's exhausting you. It's taking a toll on you. So when you feel the obligation, the need, the call, and the pull to keep watering those dead plants, it's like a heavy cinder block attached to your ankle. No matter what has happened in your past, forgive what happened and let it go.

Watering dead plants takes up precious resources.
You've got to stop watering dead plants because all that watering takes energy—the energy you need to accomplish what you're meant to do in this world. It's time to let go of shit that doesn't work. Stop

spending your time, money, thoughts, and life experiences watering these dead plants of the past—stop exhausting your resources. Stop draining your soul. You're exhausting your opportunities.

Forgive yourself for comparing yourself to other people. Stop watering that dead plant of comparison. Stop not feeling like you're not enough. Stop waiting on someone else's approval. That person is not coming to save you. That person may never approve of you. That person may never agree with you. You may never win back that person's love; you may never win back their attention; you may never win back their friendship. So you've got to stop watering that dead plant.

If you feel fatigued, if you're feeling exhausted, if you're feeling uncertain, if you're feeling confused, if you can't make decisions, these are all good indications that you're watering a lot of dead plants. For example, how many of you are busy watering a dead follow-up? It's like that person is so clearly a no; they're not going to give you a credit card. They're giving you the run around; you're dragging them around, they're dragging you around. This is a dead plant. It's clear— you can see from the roots that it is dried up and dead.

Stop telling yourself, "I keep watering them because of loneliness," or "I keep watering them because of fear," or "I keep watering them because of concern," or "I keep watering them because I hope it will change; I hope it will be different."

Remember, forgiveness is letting go of the hope that the past could have been any different.

For hurtful things that have happened in your past that may still affect you, let me be clear: Nothing is more fascinating than forgiving somebody for something they were never sorry they did. Nothing in your life will be more triumphant than forgiving somebody for something that they were never sorry they did. Nothing is more powerful. That is the ultimate in human evolution.

Dead plants don't need your attention.
They are permitting you to move on. It's time to stop watering all these dead plants because you have important work to do. There are better clients for you. There is more money for you. There are better relationships for you, better friendships for you. There are better work situations for you, better jobs for you, better businesses for you. These are all live plants, ready to grow and blossom. But you won't even see them if you're focused on what's dead at your feet. You will miss amazing opportunities because you're so busy hauling bucket after bucket of water to feed the dead plants.

It's time to start watering the right things. You have to start giving your attention to the right things. Those tiny seeds are just waiting to grow into big, beautiful, abundant gardens for every single one of you.

CHAPTER 9

Starve Fear and Feed Faith

"Fear and faith cannot coexist in our hearts at the same time."
–Neil L. Andersen

If there's ever been a time to pay attention to what's happening in our world, it's certainly been these past eighteen months. Whether it's the coronavirus pandemic, the fight for equality, weather events, or politics, there has **never** been more breaking news.

Now, I've been reading and watching and keeping up with it all like the rest of us, but let me tell you something: I am not sitting and obsessing about the news. First of all, they say the same damn thing over and over again. It's the same story. The same outrage. The same stoking of our fears. The same playing into our insecurities. There's no need to stay tuned for "breaking news" because it's essentially the same story on repeat.

You've got to limit your input.
I'm not talking about input from the people you couldn't see during times like the coronavirus pandemic, who live far away from you. I'm talking about the input of negativity. Of fear. Of conversations about how awful things are or how the world will never recover.

You've got to limit the interactions and activities that breed fear. You have to develop the leadership ability to pivot conversations toward more positive outcomes.

Breaking news: but don't be the person who is detached from the news and thus irrelevant.

Pivoting conversations this way is one way to starve fear in times of uncertainty.

It has taken this challenging, crazy time for me to have an aha about how I built my business ten years ago. How did I work a sixty-hour-a-week day job and still build a side hustle of a business? How did I do it not knowing what I was doing? How did I get rid of the uncertainty and the fear? And it's taken this crazy year for me to get it. *I starved the fear. I starved the fear, and in its place, I fed it faith.*

Fear breaks things down. Faith builds things up. It's just that simple. What you place your focus on grows, so if all you do is spend time focusing on the things that scare you, that's all you will see. But on the flip side, when you feed faith, when you focus on the things that will help you grow and move in the direction of your goals, wonderful things happen.

Five Ways to Starve Fear and Feed Faith
1. Become a master at pivoting conversations to what both parties need, even if the other party isn't aware that they need it.

It's all too easy to focus on what is going wrong. Most people want an opportunity to vent. To whine. To talk about what is going wrong.

It's okay if a conversation starts that way. Next comes the skill of channeling that conversation in a positive direction—one based on what they need.

What people need right now is an idea.

What they need right now is support.

What they need right now is the space to breathe.

What they need right now is encouragement.

What they need right now is the reminder that whatever they are struggling with is a short-term problem.

In 2020, we didn't experience an economic challenge because there was a lack of demand. There was no lack of demand. The economy was in great shape. We were doing really well. We experienced an economic challenge because we had a health crisis—and continued to have one. So the demand was there, but it was pent up. So the bottom line is that we faced a short-term challenge. And that's the perspective we need. Starve any other conversation.

It is your moral obligation. It is your leadership responsibility to starve all the negative, panic-ridden conversations. It is your obligation for who you are and how you want to lead people, and who you want to be for your family and your business and for your life, to starve out fear-based conversations. That is how you feed faith.

That doesn't mean you don't listen to someone who is in pain. That doesn't mean you don't support someone or help someone who is challenged right now or feeling alone or feeling isolated. But then you pivot that conversation to what you both need.

Remember, you have the power to suffocate fear. If you don't give it light, if you don't provide it with air, it will not persist if you don't provide it with water. It will not grow. It will not be present in your life. It will not be present in your conversations. So starve fear, suffocate fear—and feed faith.

2. Starve fear in your business and your sales.

I was on a call recently with some phenomenal leaders that included just about every name that has ever been a *New York Times* bestselling author in the business space or the personal development space. One person on the call said, "I just don't know that you can sell right now." Immediately I thought, "Starve that fear! Suffocate that fear because people need things right now."

Now, it's true that when significant changes happen globally, we have to alter our approach. We have to be compassionate and have empathy. We have to understand that not everybody is in a space right now to buy. So yes, your conversations have to be intelligent and empathetic and caring. But if you think that right now, this is a time for you to sit and do nothing, you're wrong.

Fear is contagious, and nowhere is that more dangerous than in business. Imagine what would happen if I showed up to work and told my team, "Well, guys, I don't know what we're going to sell right now because all hell is breaking loose." I can promise you the next thing *they* would do is polish up their resume because if the boss is scared, everyone should be too.

3. Up-level your relationships.

When the pandemic hit, it became evident that all we truly have is our relationships. We were social-distancing and quarantining, stuck in our homes and isolating. And yet, relationships are what kept us going.

Feed faith by doubling up on relationship-building. Relationships are a virtuous cycle: The more you are in a relationship, the more you are building relationships, the more you're reaching out to people, the more you are asking questions, the more faith you will build, and the less room there will be for fear. Creating better relationships creates reciprocity, faith, and trust.

4. Drop your fear on the floor so we can all stomp on it.

This requires some vulnerability. This requires openness to be able to stand proudly and say, "This is my fear. What's yours? This is where I worry. Where do you worry?" When we have a lot going on, and it all feels like too much, the best thing to do is dump your fears on the floor so you can suffocate them. You can't suffocate what you were too afraid to talk about. You can't starve what you pretend doesn't exist. So bring it into the open, announce it loud, and then…stomp the ever-living shit out of it.

That's how you do it. You don't hang on to it. You don't harbor it. You don't let it eat you up inside. You don't let it become a fear that you are feeding. You don't let it fester and fester and get bigger and bigger. You throw it down, and we all suffocate it together because you are not alone. You are only alone when you isolate what's going on for you. You are only alone when you isolate the challenges that you're having.

Let's get busy starving our fears.

Let's focus on suffocating our fears.

Let's support each other, lift each other up, and starve each other's fears. Let's feed each other's faith so we can pivot and keep from feeling like nothing is going to work.

5. Work your ass off right now.

This was part of my big aha about how I got over my own fear, the significant insight into how I got to where I am today. I became disciplined and so focused that anytime the fear would come up, I'd say to myself, "Put another hour in." Anytime the fear would come up, I'd write another to-do list; I'd write a brainstorm list. I highly recommend this. Who have you not talked to? Who have you not reached out to? Who have you not emailed? Who have you not called? Who have you not texted?

You can starve fear by working your butt off right now. It's impossible to be in fear and also be in action. It's impossible to do both at the same time. Be in action! Be in work mode. Be in idea mode. Be in "I don't know if this is going to work, but I'm going to try it" mode. Be in the "I'm throwing spaghetti against the wall to see if it sticks" mode. Say to yourself, "Let's just try this one thing. Let's just call this one person. Let's just post this one thing."

Because the fascinating thing is…when you work your ass off, the fear almost always gets snuffed out.

Fear is easy. Faith is hard.
Let's say someone hands me ten thousand oysters and tells me that ten of those oysters contain a million-dollar pearl. Full of faith, I begin to open them. Phew, I quickly discovered that oysters are hard to open. One, two, three, four, and still no pearl. *Shit.* Five, six. *Ouch!* I cut my hand. This is really hard. Seven, eight, nine, ten. Still no pearl. *This is so frustrating.* Actually, this is a stupid idea. There are obviously no pearls in any of these. I hate oysters. I don't even want a million dollars.

Before you know it, the faith is gone, even though with each opened oyster, the chance of finding that million-dollar pearl increases.

Faith is tested when things get hard. It's tested when we are afraid and when our perfectly laid plans don't work out so perfectly.

But faith doesn't depend on things going as planned.

True faith is continued belief in the face of adversity. True faith is continued belief in the face of fear.

It's staying strong and resilient even when you have every single reason in the world to feed your fear.

It's simple, but it isn't easy.

But you can do it.

CHAPTER 10

One Lousy Voice

"You have enemies? Good. That means you've stood up for something, sometime in your life."
– Winston Churchill

When times are challenging, it's essential to keep yourself at the level of energy you need to be at to work through the obstacles and challenges—to do what you just usually do daily while there is chaos going on in our world. You can plan your day and be prepared to implement your strategies and take the proper action steps, but one voice, one singular negative voice, can begin to tear all that down.

In this chapter, I'm going to share with you how not to let that happen.

The New Abnormal

One thing that became clear during 2020 is that our challenges and fears often change from day to day. They sometimes change from hour to hour. So we need to make sure we know how to stay positive and continue working and moving forward despite the current situation we find ourselves in.

Let me acknowledge this: Some of our fears are real, some of them manufactured, and many of them are actualized in what's going on. But they're all present.

By the time this book has been published, life in many ways will have gone back to "normal." But the reality is that life will never go back to normal, not go back to how it was before the world experienced a global health crisis. And there is real grief about the loss of what 2020 was supposed to look like. This was a temporary situation, but it doesn't mean it wasn't challenging. We've all been forced to navigate certain things we've never done before. Maybe you've always done things offline, but now you're learning to do things online for the first time. We're learning to be resilient. We're showing up, looking for the positive, and keeping our eyes open for new opportunities. We're learning grit, and we're learning to be scrappy. We're starting fresh every day, and we're making sure our mindset is strong. We're learning to pivot.

And while we're all working so hard to keep things afloat, stay positive, and interact more with people than we have ever before—the flipside of this is that just one voice can destroy what we're building.

I have an obligation to get up and lead a team of people every day. These people have rents to pay and car payments, and children to feed. It is my job to say, "Moving forward, what can we do today?" My clients are looking to me for advice; they are looking to me for leadership. They are looking to me for what we can do today and what's next tomorrow. They are looking to me to tell them how we can get through this. And that's what I do daily. I'm human, so I have my moments, but I make sure I'm revving myself up and revving you up.

But I am not a Pollyanna. My head is not in the sand saying, "This is okay." Because, damn it, this is *not* okay. This sucks; this is hard. People are losing money, losing jobs, losing their lives. People have shut down their businesses, millions have been laid off, and we have skyrocketing numbers of people whom COVID-19 struck down. This is not okay, but it's where we are. It's what we've been handed, and we can't give it back. It's all we've got right now. This disruption has happened, this chaos has happened, this health crisis has happened, and it's what we have now. And now we have to take a big pile of shit and figure out how to make a shit pie—a tasty shit pie at that. That's what we have to do right now.

So get your aprons on, get your rolling pins out, pull out the sugar in the pantry—and start realizing it's time for us to get baking. It's an imperfect world, and it's time for us to turn this shit into a shit pie. That's how we'll be able to move forward; that's how we'll be able to move our businesses forward.

I've been criticized for doing just that—moving my business forward. I've been attacked online for acting like it's "business as usual"—for acting as if nothing is wrong. Notice I used the word *criticized*, as in receiving criticism and not feedback.

Feedback is one thing—feedback is valuable even when it's hard to hear.

Criticism is something else.

Hillary Rodham Clinton famously said, "You have to take criticism seriously, but not personally." This is an important distinction. When someone is telling you something negative, they're not giving you feedback; they're criticizing you. They're criticizing you because they're threatened by the fact that you're moving forward, you're trying to be in a good place, you're strategizing and working.

When one voice is saying, "You're wrong. You're wrong for moving forward. This is worse than you think; there's no moving forward," they are not having a conversation with you. They are not giving you feedback; *they are criticizing you for moving forward.* They are attacking you for being a voice of reason, and you have to cut that off at its knees; you cannot take it in right now.

This doesn't mean that you don't listen to people. It doesn't mean that you don't meet people where they are. If somebody is struggling and in a bad place and feeling negative today, you can support them. You can help them, but if they are committed to being negative, they are criticizing you, and you better get out of that space; you better get out of that energy. So when I was criticized for acting like it's business as usual, I paused and listened. I said, "I'm going to take this seriously, but not personally." I took that criticism seriously, and as a result, I concluded, "Okay, I don't have a magic ball, and neither do they."

Negativity is a seriously lousy voice.
Lousy voices can come from everywhere. From the news. From social media. From neighbors. And while, to some extent, you can insulate

yourself from certain voices, there are others you may not be able to shut out so easily…the people you're talking to and the people you're surrounding yourself with. So when those voices creep up, you have to do everything you can to either ignore it or, even better, pivot the conversation into a positive direction.

So who are your negative voices? Maybe it's a friend, or a family member, or a client, a colleague, a boss. It could also be a news channel, a website, a Facebook group. Whatever that one voice is, take a stand. "I will not allow one voice to take me out. I will not allow one voice to destroy me. I will not allow one voice to stop what I am doing. I will not allow one voice to take me from being forward-thinking, innovative, creative, and driven. I've got to do this, we've been handed shit, and I've got to make shit pie. I won't allow this one person to deflate it."

We're going to be deflated enough as it is. Life is tough. Business is tough. But whatever is going on, we have to turn that around and see the opportunity and focus on that.

10, 10, 10
10 minutes, 10 days, 10 months
Melonie, my wife and the president of our company, has a sign in her office that says in big numbers "10, 10, 10." I'm going to explain what this means, but first, let me say that it will absolutely change your life if you live by this. It's perfect for the times we're living through right now, but it will change your life no matter what the situation is. So here's how it breaks down:

- What do I need to be successful and protect my business and my family in the next 10 minutes?
- What do I need to protect my business and my family in the next 10 days?
- What do I need to protect my business and my family for the next 10 months?

It's 10 minutes, it's 10 days, and it's 10 months. So we've got to be thinking in terms of 10, 10, 10 right now.

In the next 10 minutes, what do I need? What needs to happen? Who do I need to be around? What voice do I need to hear? What voice do I need to cut out?

In the next 10 days, what action do I need to take? What do I need to focus on? Where does my energy need to go?

For the next 10 months, what does that look like? None of us have a perfect calendar right now; none of us have a magic ball. We don't have a magic eight ball right now that we can shake and then say, "Tell me what you see today."

But we can move forward. We can move forward and think about 10 minutes, 10 days, and 10 months. 10 minutes, 10 days, 10 months— all those all look different. What I need in the next 10 minutes will look different from what I need in the next 10 days, and what I need in the next 10 days will look different from what I need in the next 10 months.

And if we can keep that mindset, that one voice won't destroy us.
So think about that one voice in your own life. Each of you reading
this knows the voice you've got to clear out right now. You know the
voice you need to eliminate right now. You can love that person, you
can support that person, you can send beautiful white light to that
person, but that voice is not helping you right now, so write in your
journal or somewhere where you will see it: "I will not allow that one
voice to destroy me."

All we've got right now is the situation we're in, and all we can do is
move forward through it and innovate from it. You can do a fantastic,
beautiful job of that, so do not allow one voice to destroy you. Instead,
live by the 10, 10, 10 rule, and watch your life change!

CHAPTER 11

The Victim in You Will Destroy the Warrior in Me

"Life doesn't victimize us, we do that to ourselves."
-Sayings

Shit's about to get real. You ready?

We're about to go what I call "under the under," which is getting into what's going on beneath the surface for many of us. In the last chapter, we talked about the harmful effects of "one lousy voice." And while I spoke about how to insulate yourself from those lousy voices, I want to go even deeper and talk about what's behind the lousy voice and how it can mess you up.

What's behind the lousy voice? Victim energy.

I remember when the pandemic first hit in 2020. Everyone was thrown off. And although we were all scared, in so many ways, we pulled together. We helped each other rise up. But as time went on and we found ourselves taking those first few steps back toward normalcy, I noticed a sea change in how people showed up. It was like their energy began to change. People seemed to be angrier, more frustrated. All the pent-up anxiety, isolation, loss of income, perceived loss of opportunity resulted in what I can only call "victim energy."

Victim energy is essentially a negative cloud that hangs around anyone in a perpetual state of belief that everything in their life is happening to them, versus them affecting what takes place. You know these people. It's someone else's fault they can't get clients. It's someone else's fault they aren't taking care of their health. It's someone else's fault for everything.

Please, please; before you send me an angry email telling me how insensitive I am, let me be perfectly clear: There are actual victims in all of this—there are people who got sick; they are victims of the coronavirus. People lost their jobs and had financial challenges due to the coronavirus and what it did to our economy. So I'm not saying that there aren't any victims, but what I am saying is that we have to learn to deal with what I call "victim energy."

Under the under

I've learned some positive ways to deal with victim energy. It's all about understanding how to have conversations with people and meet people where they are.

Under the under is what's happening or being said, and then what's going on under that.

At the root of victim energy is something we've been talking about nonstop throughout this book—people are afraid. They are frustrated, and they feel stumped.

And while it's all well and good for *other* people to have victim energy, the problem is this: The victim energy in you can destroy the warrior in me. When people are stressed, many of them use stress as a pathway for excuses, for victimhood. They are using the stress to make you wrong, make you bad, make you ugly, make you not what they can't be right now.

To put the danger of victim energy in context: When the pandemic hit, my company started an online forum called "The More Than OK Club," which we used to keep our community connected and offer insights, teaching, and support. My wife, Melonie, said something that illustrates this. She said, "You know, Suzanne, when you started the club, people were so grateful for everything our team was doing and all the extra time you were putting in and the hours of content you were making available." But then she went on to say, "There will come a time where that will turn into making you wrong. There will be some people who will accuse you of using this for something other than it is."

And she was right. While I was hard at work getting the club up and running, a family member sent me an email that essentially said, "This is the most disgusting thing I've ever seen anybody do—telling people that things are going to be OK in a time when people are dying and losing their jobs. You've really missed the mark here, and I'm embarrassed for you."

Now, had I been in a different place, I could've let that destroy me. I didn't respond to that email because I got where that person was coming from. That person was afraid of being affected by the pandemic. That person was suffering their suffering. I wasn't; I was problem-solving. But while I could not let this affect me, it could've easily derailed me and stopped me in my tracks. And that's because I had something in place—a protective bubble.

Create a bubble of protection around you.
Listen, you'll encounter scenarios like this as well, and so you have to protect yourself. Every single one of you reading this needs to put a bubble around you. This is one of the most incredible things you can do for yourself. And this is something that if you share this concept with your clients, with your family, with your customers, with your colleagues, everyone is so much richer for it.

You need to create a protective bubble because if you allow the victim in, someone else to destroy the warrior in you, you both lose. The moment I let the victim in you destroy the warrior in me, thousands of people suffer.

People are never going to like everything you do; you can't please everybody. People will be annoyed by your problem-solving and your optimism, and how you look for opportunities in challenging times. That's going to annoy people who are victims and people who need to suffer.

Do you notice that victims do not suffer in silence? Victims suffer in public because they need the attention of being the victim.
I want you to step into vulnerability and honestly reflect on when you have been a victim in the last twelve months. What has it looked like?

Have you said to your team or your spouse that you have to do it all alone?

Have you told a coach or a colleague that you just can't do this because times are too hard?

Have you thrown up your hands at some point and said, "I need somebody else to save me"?

When you can acknowledge the victim in yourself and recognize how that victimhood is not serving you and how it's never going to move you forward and how it's never going to help you, you will also begin to see the victimhood in other people. That's when you will put a bubble around you, and you will not allow the victimhood in somebody else to destroy the warrior in you.

When you acknowledge the victim in you, you can suppress it. You can eliminate it because you can know that it is your weakest self.

You have to know that when you are a victim, you are powerless.
I mentioned earlier what victimhood was like in other people. But what does it look like in you?

- It's not my fault.
- I can't go on.
- It's worse for me.
- Woe is me. I can't do this.
- How did I end up here?
- Why is this happening to me?
- Why is this happening to the world?
- Why is this happening to my neighbor?

When you allow a victim to hang around in your space, you begin to diminish your warrior.
When you allow someone to stay in a victim place:

- someone you have to listen to
- you have to witness
- you have to watch
- you have to serve
- you have to coach because they're a client of yours
- you have to love because they're a family member

When you allow them to stay in a victim's place—your warrior power diminishes.

If you want to succeed in business, you have to be a warrior. So we fight every day; we do battle every day. We do what we're supposed to do every day!

When victims show up, we walk away.
When victims show up, we take some time to remember that we are warriors, and they either can join us in war, or they'll have to move to the sidelines. This may sound harsh, but you cannot take care of every victim who is unwilling to give up their victimhood.

Many of my clients love to save people. We love helping people, and now there are so many people to help. But, you cannot save the victim who's not willing to get out of the victimhood. Because if you do—if you try to save them, if you hold on to them too long, if you try to work with them too long, if you try to love them too long, the victim in them will destroy the warrior in you.

You cannot afford to be defeated right now. You cannot afford to be moved right now. You cannot allow yourself to be shaken right now. So it's critical for you to have boundaries. It's critical for you to know when to walk away. It's critical for you to know when to put up the bubble around yourself. It is critical for you to recognize a victim—not only in others but in yourself—because the victim in someone else or yourself will begin to diminish the warrior in you.

It's so much easier to pull someone down than to lift someone up.
So, for example, if someone is standing on a table, and I give them my hand and say, "Pull me up on this table," it would be virtually

impossible for that person to pull me up onto that table. But one good jerk down, and I could pull that person off of that table. It is so much easier.

One of my clients came down with the coronavirus. He told me, "While I was in the hospital battling COVID-19, all I could think about was 'how do I stay alive?' I didn't think about my business at all. My main concern was staying alive. Now that I've recovered, the challenges in front of me right now aren't as big when I compare them to being in the hospital, gasping for air."

When you have to fight for something, you can only fight for what's in front of you.
You have to focus on that one thing and eliminate everything else. You cannot be a victim, and you cannot let victims be around you when you're fighting for your life. And while this client was fighting for his life, so many of you are fighting for your business life. You're fighting for your livelihood. You're fighting to make sure that you don't go backward. You have to avoid being codependent by trying to rescue or enable others. It will drain you, and nobody wins.

It's a brutal reminder that you're going to have to walk away from some people. You're going to have to walk away from some circumstances. You're going to have to walk away from some groups. You're going to have to stop listening to some family members because the warrior in you cannot take on the victim in them.

Stop right now and say out loud: "I am a warrior." (No, seriously, do it right fucking now.)

Write it in your journal.

Write it on a sticky note and put it on your computer screen.

It is the warrior in you that will suppress the victim in you.

It is the warrior in you that will remind you that you can do this, that you are doing this.

It is the warrior in you that is unstoppable and unshakable.

It is the warrior in you that cannot be knocked down.

And…most importantly, if you do get knocked down, it is the warrior in you that will get your ass back up.

You cannot be knocked down. And if you get knocked down, you will get back up.

CHAPTER 12

Everything Has Changed Except for You

"The only way to make sense out of change is to plunge into it, move with it, and join the dance."
-Alan Watts

Let me begin the ending with the obvious: Everything that happens in the world and everything that happens in our lives shapes everything that comes next. When momentous things occur, momentous change is bound to follow.

When the world experienced a global pandemic, it was a temporary, intense situation—but the ramifications and implications will have a permanent effect on the future.

I know for sure that 2020 changed everything.
People have changed many of their habits.

People changed how they worked, how their kids learned, how they lived their lives.

Many people experienced financial change. How they view the world changed.

And yet—with so much change, I'm shocked by how many people haven't changed a damn bit.

Stop and think about that.
We were given this unique moment in time, this amazing opportunity and global experience, and this global pandemic. I say "given" because I believe everything is given to us. I don't believe anything happens *to* us. I believe everything is always happening *for* us.

And so, here we are in this moment of such change, when the economy is changing, when healthcare is changing, when how we communicate is changing, when how we travel is changing—everything is changing; and yet I have seen so many people who haven't changed at all.

Before the pandemic hit, I watched as so many of you were waiting for an opportunity to change.

And yet you're still waiting now.

So many of you were hoping for a chance to change your ways.

And yet, you're still hoping now.

Stop resisting change.
When everything around you is changing, you are forced to change. Unless you fight it. Unless you stay committed to staying where you are. Because if you fight that change, nothing gets better, nothing gets bigger, nothing grows.

And so, you have to ask yourself today some of the most challenging questions you will ever ask yourself in your whole life:

- What do I need to change?
- What was this a wake-up call for?
- What could this be a wake-up call for?
- What do I need to do differently every day so that my forever is better than it was before this?

Be honest with yourself and write the answers down.
You might feel shameful answering them.

You might feel guilty writing them down.

You may not want to admit the answers to yourself.

But if you can uncover the change, you need to make while everything and everyone around you is changing. So if you can step into that and experience that and if I can show you how to break through that—your life will never look the same again.

So once again:

- What do you need to change?
- What do you know you need to change?
- What change are you resisting?
- Where is the resistance coming from?
- Are you brave enough to change?

I'll be blunt: If you don't have a willingness, a hunger, to come up with answers to these questions, you've got to ask yourself if owning a business is right for you.

I can tell you that I've had to change a shitload of things. I've had to change so many damn things that I'm just about worn out and exhausted from all this damn change (and I once had an event called "Be the Change!").

But I keep making those changes because I know it is the only way for me to stay afloat, keep the lights on, keep my family intact, and gainfully employ my team.

When everything around you is changing, but you are standing dead in the same place as you were a year ago—you've got a real fucking problem.

Stop pivoting and start producing.
I'm sick of talking about pivoting. If I hear one more person say pivot, I'm going to puke. Pivoting is not the answer right now.

It's just another excuse for why you're not changing, and I'll tell you why.

(A quick note: I am firmly aware that chapter 8 talks about pivoting in the context of "pivoting a conversation." This is entirely different.)

Stop thinking that you need to pivot. It just gives you another reason to stop, another reason not to call people, another reason not to move forward. And this reason—is just an excuse.

If you just got energized to do what you should've done a long time ago—and even if you did it now without any pivot involved—my God, there would be a miracle in your life. There would be a miracle in your bank account. There would be a miracle with the clients you work with. There would be a miracle for your family and your home and for the impact you made in the world.

This isn't about pivoting. This is about doing. It's about planting yourself firmly in the ground and saying, "I will do what I need to consistently every single day to get the result that I want to get— because to get something I have never had will require me to do something I have never done."

You don't need to pivot. You need to produce.
I want you to be a producing machine.

I want you to produce content.

I want you to produce leads.

I want you to produce sales conversations.

I want you to produce opportunities.

I want you to produce flexible moments and offers to people so they can say yes to them.

I want you to produce amazing transformations for people.

I want you to produce your own transformation.

I want you to be a producer.

You don't need to pivot. You need to produce.

Everything around you is changing.
Everybody around you is changing.

Every idea is changing.

Everything we knew is changing—yet you are still standing there full of excuses.

Pivot is just another excuse to stop.

Pivot is just another excuse to wait.

Pivot is just another excuse to say, "I'm not ready. I've got to figure it out. I need somebody to tell me what to do. I need somebody's approval. I need somebody's validation."

IT'S TIME TO CHANGE

I don't mean change who you are or change your business. I mean change your behaviors and your action.

It's time to say, "Today, I'm going to do double what I did yesterday. Today I'm going to finally get up and do that one thing I've been talking about for the past six months because it's enough already."

You have to decide what you are doing, how you are being, and who you are—matters in this world.

I want you to get that deep in your very being. I want you to dig deep into yourself and understand that you don't need to pivot. You need to produce. And most importantly, you have every capability of producing—because you matter, and what you do matters.

You don't need validation, you don't need certification, and you don't have to know it all. You don't have to be perfect; you don't have to look amazing. You just need to show up. Because somebody needs you. Somebody is waiting for you.

But here's the problem. You are not willing to change.

You are not willing to give up being comfortable so that you can have everything you've ever wanted in your life.

You are not willing to give up not being embarrassed.

You're not willing to give up the safety of "If I don't go out there, if I don't put me out there, if I don't show up, then I can't be shamed."

There is only success in shaming because you will feel ashamed.

You will be ashamed.

Someone will try to shame you.

Because that's what comes with success.

That's what comes with showing up.

And you have to find the courage to not fear being shamed.

What you do matters, but it requires you to change.
It doesn't require you to pivot.

It doesn't require you to tweet.

It doesn't require you to be new in a new world.

You don't need to be new in a new world. You need to be *you* in the world.
The world is constantly changing. It was changing before the global pandemic of 2020. It has been changing during it, and it's going to continue to change long after it. You need to be you in the world, and

for every moment you wait, for every day you wait, you suffocate your service to others.

This is hard work. I have never lied about that.

I have never hidden that from anybody. But you wouldn't be reading this if you didn't want to do that work and didn't want to make a difference. You are here for a reason. I am here for a reason. People need you; they are in pain, and they are in suffering, and they are in trauma, and they are in drama, and they need help. And you know what? They were in pain even before the world got turned upside down.

It is not that different, except that the world is changing and you're not willing to.

If you indeed are in the same place today, when all this started, are you stuck? No, you're not stuck. You're stubborn. You don't want to change. You don't want a business. You don't want to grow a business. You don't want clients. You don't want financial freedom. You are happier being where you are despite the pain you are experiencing than you are hungry for freedom.

You are happier in the pain that you know than the freedom you don't know.

Here's the funny part—I'm not asking you to make significant, sweeping changes to every aspect and every behavior in your life. Instead, I'm talking about the tiny changes every single day that put you one step closer to your dreams and helping other people have their dreams as well. You don't need to be a new you in a new world. You need to be *you* in the world. That's what matters today.

So yes, it feels as if everything around us has changed and is changing. That's because it is. And so you have to ask yourself in this time of great change: "Am I willing to change?" Because if you genuinely want to be the change you wish to see in the world, it starts with you. It begins with your daily habits. It begins with your behaviors. It begins with your commitment level, and it starts with your drive. So, everything is changing, but you don't need to change who you are or what you do. You just need to change how consistently you're doing it—because the world is waiting.

Having the courage to change is all that matters now. Taking one new daily action every day is all that matters now. That's how you change your life. That's how you change others' lives.

And that's how you win, no matter what.